The Legend of the
Green Gorilla

Copyright © 2021 Sean Woolford

All rights reserved. No part of this book may be reproduced in any form or by any electronic or mechanical means, including information storage and retrieval systems, without permission in writing from the publisher, except by reviewers, who may quote brief passages in a review.

ISBN 978-1-7371404-0-5 Paperback
ISBN 978-1-7371404-1-2 Hardcover
Library of Congress Control Number: 2021910063

Publisher's Cataloging-in-Publication data
Names: Woolford, Sean, author. | Thompson, Chad, 1974-, illustrator.
Title: The legend of the green gorilla / story by Sean Woolford ; pictures by Chad Thompson. Description: Gilbert, AZ: Green Gorilla Books, 2021. | Summary: Two brothers search for a mythical fifty- foot-tall green gorilla. When they ignore the signs warning "Do Not Touch", a game of cat and mouse begins
Identifiers: LCCN: 2021910063 | ISBN: 978-1-7371404-1-2 (hardcover) |
978-1-7371404-0-5 (paperback) | 978-1-7371404-2-9 (ebook)
Subjects: LCSH Brothers--Juvenile fiction. | Animals, Mythical--Juvenile fiction. | Adventure and adventurers--Juvenile fiction. | Humorous stories. | CYAC Brothers--Fiction. | Animals, Mythical--Fiction. | Adventure and adventurers--Fiction. | BISAC JUVENILE FICTION / Action & Adventure / General | JUVENILE FICTION / Animals / Apes, Monkeys, etc. | JUVENILE FICTION / Family / Sibling | JUVENILE FICTION / Humorous Stories
Classification: LCC PZ7.1.W6655 Leg 2021 | DDC [E]--dc23

Printed in United States of America
Published by Green Gorilla Books
Visit greengorillabooks.com for more information

For Eva, Michael and all other young storytellers:
Always look out for life's adventures.

Not long ago, in a town close to you
Lived a young boy named
Mark and his big brother **Stu**.

They heard many stories, the myths and tall tales
Of a **giant gorilla** as big as a whale.

They sailed to an island in a neighboring lake Unaware that their journey would be a mistake.

"We've heard that he lives here. I hope it's not true."
"It's a fake. Just a story. Not real!" chuckled Stu.

Mark wasn't as calm as his big brother seemed.
To him, it all started to feel like a dream.

On the island, a trail led them deep through the trees.
A posted sign warned them,
Don't touch the ape, please.

Go back! Do Not Enter! Seriously!

One sign read,
Go Back! You shouldn't be here!
The boys figured there was
still nothing to fear.

But they stopped in their tracks
when they saw the big cave.
Mark started to panic.
He didn't feel brave.

The cave was enormous and totally dark.

"Good thing I brought flashlights."
Stu tossed one to Mark.

Don't Touch!
We Mean It!
FOR REAL!

The bright light reflected a cage made of steel.
One last sign read: "Don't touch! We mean it! For real!"

In the cage was an ape that was big as a wall.

Twenty- no, Thirty- no, **FIFTY** feet tall!

His hair - green as grass from his head to his toes.

But why was it green? We're not sure. No one knows.

The ape's eyes flew open.
He let out a

ROAR!!

A sound they had certainly not heard before.

"We need to get out of here! Quick! To the boat!"
While running, Mark wondered: "Do giant apes float?"

Another sound struck them. The bars in the cage
Were bending as the ape escaped in a rage.

They heard something rumbling.
The boys could feel doom.
Each step the ape took,
the ground shook:

BOOM!

BOOM!

BOOM!

They jumped in the boat, just a bit more secure.
"I'm not sure if it swims, but go fast to be sure."

"The water will stop him.
We'll be in the clear.
We'll sail right back home
and forget we were here."

From the boat, they could see some trees starting to fall. The ape came out running:

BOOM! BOOM! BOOM! CANNONBALL!

They pedaled so fast as they rode into town.
Their yelling and screaming
made them look like clowns.

"The big ape is coming! Go back to your rooms!"
From far off, they heard him:

BOOM! BOOM! BOOM! BOOM!

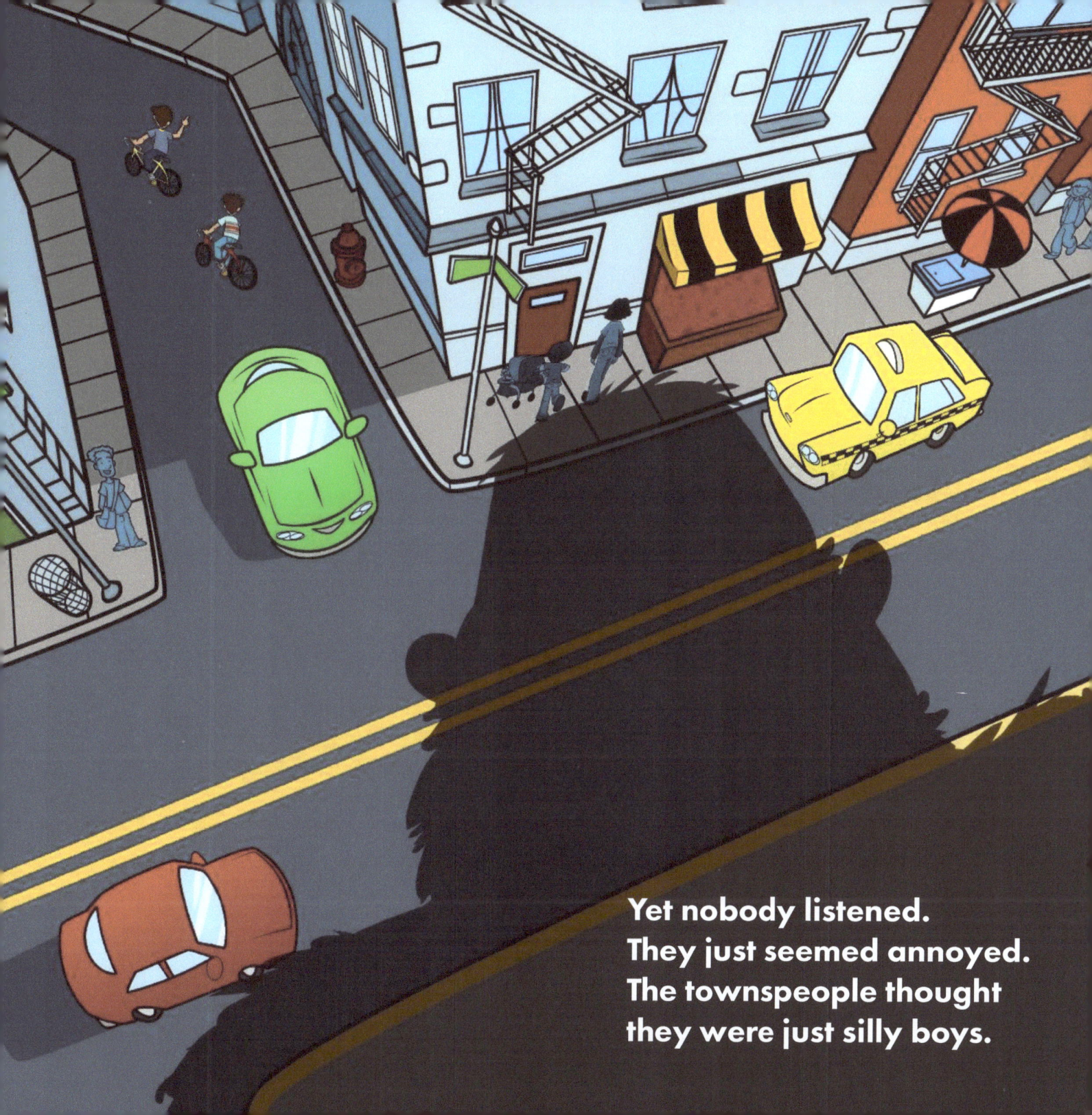

Yet nobody listened. They just seemed annoyed. The townspeople thought they were just silly boys.

While biking,
Mark looked back
and saw the ape's face.
He noticed a smile
was firmly in place.

He was smiling.
Was he laughing?
To him, this was fun!
Mark looked 'round and saw
how much damage was done.

They ran to the farmhouse. They banged on the door. The gorilla was closer and down on all fours.

Mark was angry and scared as tears rolled down his cheek. When Stu saw that, he knew he should stop being weak.

Stu stepped up,
"Behind me. I'm here to save you.
It's my fault, not yours.
It's what big brothers do."

The gorilla bent over and brushed Stu aside.
Just like you would when you swat at a fly.

The mammoth beast squatted.

Mark knew this was it.

The green ape just poked him and said:

"Tag You're it."

the end

**Please visit greengorillabooks.com
for more fun and games.**

**Use the following blank pages to draw your own
giant gorilla. What color would yours be?**

CPSIA information can be obtained
at www.ICGtesting.com
Printed in the USA
LVHW070958150921
697864LV00002B/31